Meditations for the
Unemployed

Meditations for the Unemployed

Richard L. Francis

iUniverse, Inc.
New York Lincoln Shanghai

Meditations for the Unemployed

iUniverse, Inc.

For information address:
iUniverse, Inc.
2021 Pine Lake Road, Suite 100
Lincoln, NE 68512
www.iuniverse.com

Cover design by Doug Sykes
Page design by iUniverse
Edited by Theresa McGahan

ISBN: 0-595-33069-X

The journey of a thousand miles
begins and ends with one single step.

Lao Tsu
Tao Te Ching

Contents

ACKNOWLEDGEMENTS

Grateful thanks is due to my wife, Connie, whose support and encouragement in both good times and bad has made all the difference. I am also grateful to my editor, Teresa McGahan for her expert advice. Special thanks goes to Doug Sykes for his creative expertise in developing the cover design. In addition to those already mentioned, the thoughtful opinions of Dr. Dwight Neuenschwander and Ron Snell also proved to be most valuable during critical stages in the writing of the text. Finally, I wish to express a special note of appreciation to Billy Thornberg whose example has been a steadfast inspiration to me as well as many other writers.

INTRODUCTION

Every person's story is important to them. It is the history of their journey through life. My journey began in the 1930's, in the midst of the Great Depression. I was born a middle child in a chemically dependent family. My father was a traveling salesman. My mother was a stay-at-home housewife who suffered from manic depression. Not surprisingly, my first job in life was being my mother's counselor. It didn't work, but I tried my best. You might say it was training for a later role I was to play in life.

I worked as a butcher boy at a local meat market during high school. The skills I learned were to later help me earn my way through college. I attended college for one year and dropped out not knowing what I wanted to do with my life. Three years later, after stints of working as a drill press operator, ambulance attendant, and forest fire lookout, I returned to college.

This time I completed my college degree and taught social studies in five different high schools in the Midwest during the next five years. All that time, I felt I did not belong in teaching, but the path of least resistance seemed better than re-entering an uncertain job world.

Eventually I returned to college to work on a counseling degree. In the ensuing years I worked as a counselor in education, chemical dependency and finally, in mental health.

In assessing my own work history, I feel that it is typical of the work-related changes affecting many people's lives. According to the Department of Labor, the average person has three careers and ten different jobs in their lifetime. I believe that what distinguishes most people's careers is not how many jobs they have had, but how they have faced the challenges those changes bring.

Over the years I have witnessed my own as well as others' struggles with career change. Frequently, those changes have been punctuated by periods of unemployment. Like it or not, unemployment has come to be accepted as a common experience in the lives of many modern day workers. Today's unemployment figures may seem discouraging. Millions of Americans are out of work as a result of economic recession, corporate down-sizing and the off-shoring of jobs. Still, the situation is not hopeless. People are finding work and new jobs are being created.

Losing a job is extremely stressful no matter what the reason. Fear, anxiety, and worry often accompany threats to one's security. While these negative emotions are normal responses to stress, they do not have to take control of your life. There are positive measures you can take to keep your balance even under the most difficult circumstances.

Meditations for the Unemployed addresses the emotional upheaval often felt by those who have lost their job. It offers practical steps for coping during stressful times. Emphasis is placed on staying proactive and positive to counter negative thoughts and feelings. These meditations provide support and encouragement by reaffirming the value of each person's struggle to find work. The central message is one of hope. It says your time between jobs may try your patience and endurance, but you will eventually succeed in finding steady employment. You are tougher than you think. The lessons you learn from the challenges you face will not be wasted. In the end, you can emerge from your time of trial with a deeper sense of faith and purpose in your life.

My own personal experience with unemployment has convinced me that it can have far greater effects on a person's life than simply a job change. I believe God has placed each of us here on earth for a reason. Our main task, if we choose to accept it, is to fulfill His mission for us. If our Maker placed us here for a reason, then He holds the plan for our life. But we must first have a relationship with Him if we are to understand His will. It's my hope that this little book will awaken in you a fresh desire to seek a deeper relationship with the Lord.

ROADBLOCKS

o o o o o o o o o o o o o o o o o o o o o o o o o o o o o o o o o o o o o

It may be that when we no longer know what to do we have come to our real work and when we no longer know which way to go we have begun our real journey.

—*Wendell Berry*

I used to believe that I could achieve any goal I set my mind on. It took a considerable number of hard knocks to convince me otherwise. I was trained as a classroom teacher but found I had neither the patience nor the disposition to stay in education. I spent years studying counseling psychology only to find I understood myself least of all. Many of the career goals I set for myself crumbled and left me confused, angry and frustrated. My approach to self-understanding has always been trial and error. It may not be the best method, but it is one that is commonly used.

The older we grow the more apt we are to have acquired some scars from our mistakes and miscalculations. Few of us get through life without some setbacks and roadblocks along the way. When disappointments come and we are denied the fruits of our labors, we may become bitter and disenchanted with life. We have a choice to either learn from our experiences and move forward or give up on God and curse our failure to succeed. I admit to having done both. But in the end, I have always come back to the realization that bitterness only hurts me.

I believe that the roadblocks we face in life can teach us valuable lessons. God can use them to direct our path if we let Him. He may be saying, "This is not the best way for you go. Let me show you a better way."

Unemployment is one of the most serious roadblocks that a person can face. In spite of the discouragement and frustration, it may be a turning point to a new career direction. It can also offer us an opportunity to better understand God's vision for our life. The truth is, most of us do not think much about God's vision until we have lost our own.

PROTECTING YOUR MARRIAGE

Marriage with the long view comes with the conviction that nothing will break us up, that we will fight through whatever obstacles get in our way...

—*William J. Doherty*

Some wit once said, "Most marriages are made in heaven; that's why there is so much lightning and thunder in them." Whoever the author was, they forgot to include the winds of adversity as well. I should know. My own jobless times brought plenty of storms over the years. It's not much fun to tell your spouse you've lost your job. There's no getting around it, it hurts. For the most part my wife and I handled things pretty well. We learned to live on a very slim budget. Our health insurance came and went and so did many other things we once took for granted. It's amazing what "just getting by" can do for your priorities.

Perhaps the hardest lessons we learned were to be patient with each other and with God. We were slow learners, so it took us a while to catch on to this waiting business. But learn we did. We cut our budget, skimped on necessities, and made do. Thanks to my frugal wife, some meager savings and the grace of God, we managed to get by. I believe you can too. Some of the things we found helpful were:

1. Keeping our relationship with one another as a major priority in our personal lives.

2. Establishing an emergency budget as soon as I found myself out of work.

3. Setting down together to work on monthly bills and to discuss our financial needs.

4. Attending church regularly and involving ourselves in small group study programs.

5. Being willing to read and study Scripture and inspirational literature together and to pray for one another on a daily basis.

6. Agreeing to seek counseling when our marriage was facing difficult times.

7. Taking time to occasionally write out and review our marriage and personal goals together.

8. Establishing regular times when we could talk without being interrupted.

PARENTING DURING UNEMPLOYMENT

o o o o o o o o o o o o o o o o o o o o o o o o o o o o o o o o
...And this is what their father said to them when he blessed them,
giving each the blessing appropriate to him.

—*Genesis 49:28 NIV*

Parents want to be a blessing to their children. We bless our children by laboring for them and looking after their needs. Nothing brings greater pain to parents than not to being able to adequately care for their family. We feel guilty for bringing hardships upon them.

While there is no way parents can alleviate all the stresses their children face during periods of economic uncertainty, there is much we can do to head off problems. Most children are blessed with selective memories. Fortunately, they do not tend to remember the hard times of their parents later in life. What they do recall most often is the good times when family members did things together. They remember the visits to the park and playing on the swings; not how little food was in the picnic basket. We can help our children deal with our job loss in a number of ways.

1. Remember, children are not to blame for wanting things that cost money.

2. Avoid constantly saying, "We can't afford that." Instead say, "This is not the best time for such a purchase." Then ask them to think of another option that doesn't cost money.

3. Try not to argue about money matters with your spouse in front of the children.

4. Encourage your kids to use their own creative minds to come up with things to do.

5. Be aware that too much T.V. can expose your children to unnecessary wants.

6. Use low-cost church and community activities for youngsters whenever possible.

Parents should not blame themselves when unemployment brings drastic changes in family life. Children are more resilient than we realize. They will adjust pretty well to most challenges in their lives as long as their parents are all right.

The main thing you need to work at is keeping channels of communication open with your kids. Young or old, children need to feel they are a part of what's going on in their home. Holding regular family meetings lets everyone feel free to air their concerns. Listening to one another and sharing in decision making helps to reduce stress. It also builds family unity. By pulling together, your family can become even stronger during trying times.

It's important for parents to monitor their children's behavior during stressful changes in family life. Parents should be aware of any radical changes in their child's eating or sleeping habits. It's also a good idea to keep close tabs on any fluctuation in school performance. School personnel should be alerted regarding any special concerns you have about your child. Parents should not hesitate to seek professional assistance if they fear their child is showing serious symptoms of stress and depression.

GRIEF

Although the world is full of suffering, it is also full of the overcoming of it.

—Helen Keller

I once heard a minister friend of mine say, "Grieving is the hardest work there is." Grieving a job loss takes time. You may feel angry, bitter and disappointed that such a thing could be happening to you. It will take a while for your mind to realize the fact that the job is over and your life won't be the same. It's then that the grieving process begins. Be patient with yourself. Give yourself time to grieve your loss properly.

How long is it appropriate to mourn a job loss? There is no simple answer because each person may face their crisis differently. Still, it's important not to let sadness overwhelm you. Talk through your problems with a friend, spouse or counselor. Join a grief support group if one is available. Talking about your job loss can help you gain a real sense of relief and a deeper understanding of the emotional stress it has caused. Your problems will not seem so hopeless after all. You can find the strength and courage to go on.

As a counselor who has worked in mental health for many years, I'm well aware of the temptation to want to fix those who are hurting. Unfortunately, there are no easy answers for those struggling with issues of grief. Frequently all I could do was listen compassionately to the person sharing their problem. I have always been amazed at the resiliency of the human spirit. It comes through when a person who has suffered a great loss decides to pick up their life and go on with their chosen path of recovery.

TURNING POINTS IN A CAREER

○ ○

When the way comes to an end, then change. Having changed, you pass through.

—I Ching

The above passage from *I Ching* makes it sound like life changing events are easy to cope with and simple to navigate. Nothing could be further from the truth. Reaching a turning point in your career frequently means you cannot continue on the same path or go back the way you came. In times of unemployment you may have to start over, learn new skills and perfect different methods of coping.

While drastic changes in life may require adjustments, they are not impossible to survive. This country's workers have long been known for their ingenuity. We are recognized for our ability to adapt to the rapidly changing conditions of our world. Given time most of us can master any career change life thrusts upon us.

Before beginning to think about which career path to take, it is wise to consider some pertinent questions. Here is a list to help you get started with your search:

1. What career skills do I have that are saleable?

2. Do I need to gain new skills to become more employable?

3. What are my aptitudes and interests?

4. Whom do I know who can provide me with job leads?

5. Do I need to update my resume before I begin my search for work?

6. Where and when do I begin looking for employment?

TIME

What I do today is important because I am exchanging part of my life for it.

—Hugh Mulligan

The use of time in our society is often equated with earning money. It is no wonder that a person who has more time than money on his hands feels worthless. Our life and time seem devalued when they lack their previous earning power. When we are placed in the situation of being unemployed, we struggle to find new meaning in life. It takes time to regain our balance after an emotional and financial setback.

While time is no longer money to the unemployed, it is still the most valuable thing a person owns. Time is life itself. For the unemployed person, the main question is not simply, "What can I do to earn money?" but "How do I want to spend my time or my life in order to make a living?"

"What kind of job do I want?" is a career, as well as an economic question. "What shall I do with my life?" becomes a spiritual issue between you and God. It is important to ask both questions.

HAVE A PLAN

o o o o o o o o o o o o o o o o o o o o o o o o o o o o o o o o o
Therefore be careful how you walk, not as unwise men, but as wise,
but making the most of your time, because the days are evil.

—*Ephesians 5:15-16 NAS*

Much of an employed person's time is spent in the details of earning a living. Is it any wonder that a terrible vacuum is felt when a person is out of work? Suddenly we may have more time on our hands than we know what to do with. Scripture is clear. We are to be wise stewards of our time. Even when are unemployed we still have a responsibility for using our time and energy wisely.

The key to living a balanced existence during a period of unemployment is to manage time and limited resources well. In order to keep thinking straight, we need some form of a plan for short term and long term goals. How well we manage priorities regarding these goals will determine the success or failure of our daily existence as well as our job search. We can begin our list now.

1. Get a paper and pencil.

2. Write down the things you need to do today.

3. List what you want to accomplish during the coming week.

4. Ask yourself what you want to be doing a year from now. What about in five years?

MAINTAINING PRODUCTIVE ROUTINES

o o o o o o o o o o o o o o o o o o o o o o o o o o o o o o o o o o
It is the greatest mistake to do nothing because you can only do a little.

—*Sidney Smith*

One of the most difficult demands of unemployment is the continuing need to maintain orderly routines. When you are working, the job itself reinforces the need for order. With the absence of work, you are thrown back on your own resources to stay organized. The biggest challenge is how to maintain motivation and live constructively without a job.

Part of establishing a meaningful routine should include continuing to go to bed and get up at regular times. Keep regular sleep and eating habits. It will insure that you look and feel your best. Maintaining neatness and order in your personal surroundings should also be part of each day's responsibilities. Nothing drags your spirit down faster than waking up in a messy house with a sink filled with dirty dishes.

Whether it's in our personal environment or personal appearance, sloppiness works against us because it sets the tone for how each day begins and ends. The ability to maintain orderly routines is one aspect of life we all have some control over. You can begin today. Striving to establish order contributes to your morale and readiness to return to work when the time comes.

GET YOURSELF ORGANIZED

o o o o o o o o o o o o o o o o o o o o o o o o o o o o o o o o o

There are three things too much to bear:
To try to sleep and sleep not;
To love someone who loves not;
To wait for someone who comes not.

—*French Proverb*

To the above list I would add: to look for something and find not. It's hard on your self esteem and patience to have to waste time and energy looking for things that have been mislaid. Take time to get organized and work at it every day. Keep a small note book or use the computer to record names and addresses of potential employers. Don't forget to record the dates and phone numbers of job contacts. Keep accurate records. They will provide specific information that you may need later should you decide to re-contact someone.

Consistently put papers like unemployment forms and copies of job applications in a folder where you can find them. Be sure to make copies of important papers. The habit of being organized will streamline the job hunt and help provide order in your daily life. Your emotional stability as well as the efficiency of your job search will be greatly enhanced by a dependable filing system.

If you're like me, you occasionally lose track of things in spite of good intentions. What to do? I try to find a quiet place where I can sit calmly for a few minutes until I can retrace my steps since I last saw the object I am seeking. If that fails, I pretend the object is looking for me. It may not work, but you would be surprised how it relieves the mind to change your focus.

BLAMING OTHERS

For if you forgive men when they sin against you, your heavenly Father will also forgive you. But if you do not forgive men their sins, your Father will not forgive you.

—Matthew 6:14-15 NIV

It is easy to feel like a failure when we are out of work. Society constantly holds up the symbols of success which are for now temporarily beyond reach. At times, we may be thrown back on ourselves, regretting the past as well as the present. "Why couldn't I have just held onto the old job, and why did the boss let me go?" Too much introspection can lead to self incrimination and the eventual blaming of ourselves and others. If we are not careful, we may start seeing ourselves as a victim.

Victims refuse to see how holding a grudge hurts them more than the persons they blame. Somehow they feel they are getting even by holding on to resentments and bitterness. Christ recognized this all too human desire for revenge. He admonishes us to love our enemies and pray for those who persecute us. [Matthew 5:44 NIV]

It is not an easy matter to let go of a grudge. We often feel our anger is fully justified. Unfortunately, memory of the wrong keeps recycling angry emotions that can turn into bitter feelings. It may seem impossible at times to give up an old grudge but it can be done. The main thing to remember is to make a conscious effort to move on from the past. Here are some basic suggestions that can help begin the healing process:

1. Pay attention to your internal dialog so as to weed out blaming and judgmental thoughts toward yourself and others.

2. Avoid dwelling on the past in your daily conversations.

3. Keep asking God to help you let go of anger and resentment.

4. Pray for those you feel have used you spitefully.

5. Remember how much God has forgiven you.

6. Repeat the above often until all resentments are gone.

ACCEPTANCE VS. RESENTMENT

God, grant me the serenity to accept things I cannot change, the courage to change the things I can, and the wisdom to know the difference.

—The Serenity Prayer as used by Twelve Step groups

One of the most difficult steps in the journey through unemployment is to put away bitterness and accept our condition. Even when the loss of a job has been entirely unfair or seemingly unwarranted, little is gained by carrying resentments. Acceptance does not mean we are to become apathetic to our present state of unemployment. Acceptance, in a positive sense, means to turn our attention away from what cannot be changed toward present realities. Letting go of the past helps us focus on the job hunt without carrying the unnecessary baggage of hurt feelings.

Years ago I was employed in a store that sold toys and other merchandise. It was getting late in the afternoon when the boss asked me to run over to a warehouse a few blocks away to pick up a bike. On the way, I stopped briefly to grab a cup of coffee. Before I could complete the errand, the boss caught up with me and I was fired on the spot. I felt being let go was a bit extreme.

Weeks later, after much fruitless job hunting, I found work as an ambulance attendant. You can imagine my surprise when one evening we were called to pick up someone with a gall bladder attack. You guessed it. The patient was my old boss. There was a time I could have gladly strangled the guy. But ironically, I could only pity the suffering man on the pram in front of me. It would be many years before I learned the true value of acceptance, but perhaps that incident was a small beginning in my understanding of what it means to let go of the desire to get even.

Acceptance is not a despairing attitude of defeat, but a positive step that frees us to live fully in the present. Acceptance is surrender to the fact that, while the past cannot be changed, we can still find hope and courage to live in the reality of the present. Pray for acceptance today. It is the pathway to both emotional healing and peace of mind.

ANGER

Cease from anger, and forsake wrath; Do not fret, it leads only to evil doing.

—Psalm 37: 8 NAS

Anger is a normal response to being placed in a tough situation and feeling powerless over crucial aspects of our life. Since we who are unemployed are often reminded of our helplessness, it is easy for frustration to build up. It is one thing to say that anger is a normal response to anything that constantly threatens our security, but quite another to excuse it. Hostile feelings, when uncontrolled, can be very damaging to our relationships with others. Guard against allowing anger to be expressed in explosive, unhealthy ways. Here are some of the methods which are suggested as a means of coping with anger:

1. Don't brood on the past and don't attempt to blame others for your condition.

2. Find someone you can talk with and avoid unloading frustration on family members.

3. Keep busy. Make lists of daily goals and stay on task until they are completed.

4. Walk and exercise regularly in order to work off unspent energy.

5. Get involved in helping others. It will take your mind off yourself.

6. Read positive literature every day that champions an optimistic outlook of faith.

7. Make a frustration list. By all means go to work on those things you can do something about. Cross off and forget the things that are beyond your control.

8. Join a support group for the unemployed in your community, if one exists.

9. Seek professional counseling if angry or depressed feelings threaten your health.

10. Practice gentleness in your relationships. This means letting go of the tendency to say and do things that hurt others.

11. Keep a journal of daily activities. Journaling can give you a broader perspective of your present condition. It will remind you that even the toughest days don't last.

12. Take time to pray and meditate daily in order to become more calm and focused.

LOSING YOUR FEARS

o o o o o o o o o o o o o o o o o o o o o o o o o o o o o o o o o o o

When I was in distress, I sought the Lord; at night I stretched out my untiring hands and my soul refused to be comforted.

—Psalm 77:2 NIV

You are bound to feel fearful when you are thrown out of work. Whether we were expecting to be laid off or not, it is still unsettling. The loss of a job can lead to panic because of economic concerns for the future. Keeping your balance in times of uncertainty can be a struggle. The main thing is not to let unreasonable fears rule your life.

Here are some steps that can help you stay calm during tough times. First, admit you are afraid. There is no use denying you are worried. Second, analyze those fears. Try to be as specific as possible. You may be afraid of being out of work, but what you really fear is the loss of your home, marriage and prestige. Third, discuss your concerns with a good listener who can help you sort out exaggerated fears. Fourth, get busy working on plans for finding a job. There is nothing like physical activity to get your mind moving in a positive direction.

Finally, remember who is the guardian of your life. Psalm 46: 1-2 says: "God is our refuge and strength, a very present help in trouble. Therefore we will not fear though the earth be removed, and the mountains be carried into the midst of the sea." God promises to assist those who seek his help. You can trust Him to keep his promise.

WORRIES

Some days worries have a tendency to eat us alive. We may even wake up with aches and pains from worrying in our sleep. Worry erodes our self esteem and confidence. Like an acid, it eats its way into our sense of well being and gives justification to our worst fears. Soon we start thinking that nothing will work out right. The feeling of being overwhelmed is usually a sign that we are trying to solve too many problems on our own.

Painful fears and worries are an indication we have lost our feeling of closeness to our Lord. As James 4:8 reminds us, "Come near to God and He will come near to you." Reading the Bible daily, regular worship, and frequent prayer are some of the best ways to maintain our conscious contact with God. When we reach out to God, He reciprocates by restoring our hope and our faith in Him and in the goodness of life.

A strong faith is a must if we are to keep our balance in today's turbulent world. Our faith in God enables us to believe there is always something we can do to make our situation better. Faith helps us find the courage to think and act in positive ways. It encourages us to hope and believe in the return of a better day. We must fight the tendency to lose hope. Here are a few suggestions that can be useful in your fight to stay the course:

1. Spend time reading God's word. It can help you find strength and courage for meeting each day's demands.

2. Recognize that there is a difference between anxious worry and healthy concern.

3. Pray for wisdom in distinguishing the parts of your life you can control and those you can't.

4. Get enough sleep. Problems appear bigger when you are tired.

5. Take on your problems one day at a time. Troubles often seem more manageable if you tackle them one by one on a daily basis.

QUESTIONS

Some questions I should never let into my mind if I want to be happy are: What if? How come? and Why me?

—Author Unknown

Some questions are unhealthy because they are a waste of time and lead to self pity. For instance, the question of "Why me, God?" could just as easily be asked, "Why not me?" Why do I think I am above the suffering and pain any more than other human beings? By comparison, healthy questions focus on the here and now. They examine present realities and what might be done to improve our condition.

1. What is my present economic situation?

2. What job options are available at the present time?

3. Do I need some professional advice or assistance?

4. What measures do I need to take to start my job search?

5. Whom can I contact for recommendations?

6. How can I organize my time wisely as I search for work?

These are the kind of questions that get us up and moving. They are healthy questions because they focus on the present and the role we must play to achieve our goal of finding a job.

SELF PITY

Self pity, simply defined, means feeling sorry for yourself. While few of us want to admit to indulging in this negative emotion, it is hard to avoid during times of unemployment. Self pity feeds on feelings of being alone and abandoned. We may start to feel like martyrs who have been singled out for unjust treatment.

Self pity is a normal response to being thrown out of work. At first the feeling of being victimized by the system or your former employer may even seem comforting. But staying stuck in regret is counter productive. It pulls down your morale and makes you susceptible to depression. While negative feelings are tempting when you are down on your luck, there are ways to avoid becoming trapped in this self defeating cycle.

1. Become aware of your emotions. Fight the impulse to dwell on your own personal miseries.

2. Remind yourself that you are not alone and that others also share in the same condition.

3. Remember to be grateful for all your blessings. It's hard to feel sorry for yourself and grateful at the same time.

4. Get involved in helping those who are less fortunate.

5. Ask God to relieve you of preoccupation with your own troubles.

6. Consider all the things that have gone right for your life.

REGRET

Regret is an appalling waste of energy; you can't build on it; it's only good for wallowing in.

—*Katherine Mansfield*

I don't know about you, but I hate admitting my mistakes. When I mess up it's even harder to let go of them. I keep beating up on myself for not avoiding the pitfall in the first place. Many of those mistakes have contributed to my own jobless times.

My wife can usually tell when I'm indulging myself in remorseful brooding. My whole attitude turns sour. At some point she wisely interrupts my pity party by saying "You have my permission to forgive yourself." Her humorous comment usually wakes me up to the fact that I do have a choice. I can either learn from my mistake and move on, or I can keep wallowing in regret.

Sometimes we feel like such failures. We have failed to be prepared for the future. Instead of riding out the waves of change, we are now forced into an unpleasant situation as though we need to relearn something.

It's one thing to see how our choices may have contributed to our jobless condition. It's quite another to beat ourselves up for not having been able to predict the future. Second guessing ourselves is an old perfectionist blame game that only keeps us angry at ourselves and others. Resentment and blame focus our attention on the past rather than on the present, where our mind needs to be. Forgiving ourselves for short sightedness is an essential, mature approach to living free of self abasement and regret. Today we can begin by letting go of our regrets. It's perfectly all right to forgive yourself.

ENVY

o o o o o o o o o o o o o o o o o o o o o o o o o o o o o o o o o o o o o o o

Let us not become boastful, challenging one another, envying one another.

—Galatians 5: 26 NAS

It's tempting to envy those who still hold jobs when we are unemployed. We feel ostracized and cut off from a meaningful existence because we do not share in the prosperity of the larger society. Such feelings may seem justifiable, but nothing is apt to make us more miserable than comparing ourselves with others. Envy of those still working can lead to a defensive and destructive form of self pity. We feel we have been singled out and found wanting.

What can we do to avoid the demeaning effects of jealousy and envy? We can begin by developing an attitude of gratitude in our daily lives. This may seem difficult at first, but by focusing on what we have to be thankful for we are less likely to feel victimized by our jobless condition. How does one develop an attitude of gratitude when faced with hardships? An old trick suggests that you throw your shoes under your bed each night. In the morning, while you are on your hands and knees looking for your shoes, take time to give thanks for the many good things in your life.

Another approach, frequently recommended, is to write out a list of at least five things you have to be grateful for each evening. By adding new items to your list each day you slowly become more aware of the richness of life.

The practice of being grateful is just the remedy to weed out the evils of envy and resentment. Humbly thanking God for all His blessings reminds us how much we depend on Him for everything that supports our life. It also helps free our mind from the burdens of jealousy and envy.

VALUE CLARIFICATION

○ ○

Do not store up for yourselves treasures on earth, where moth and rust destroy, and where thieves break in to steal. For where your treasure is, your heart will be also.

—Matthew 6:19 and 21 NIV

Christ warns us against putting our trust in material things. Yet most of us have closets, attics, and garages filled with stuff. They are things we seldom use and that we could easily get along without. Is it need or is it greed that keeps us hanging onto our stuff? I know how it is. We tell ourselves we just might need that thing up on the shelf gathering dust. Meanwhile, the dust gets thicker on our prized possessions each year.

A period of joblessness often forces us to reexamine what's important. Living through lean times not only helps us clarify what we value, but how much we value it. For example, we may find it necessary to sell off personal belongings in order to buy food. In the process of survival we quickly learn what is most important to us.

Christ's admonition against hoarding reminds us we need to keep our priorities straight. I believe He wants us to be able to enjoy some of the good things in life. But He warns us not to let those things crowd out God's place in our heart. It can be saddening to see something we once valued sell for a few cents on the dollar. I once sold a nearly new typewriter for a third of its original cost. While I hated to let it go for that amount, I was grateful for the fact that I had something to sell.

My philosophy on how to let go of stuff is this: If what I need to sell is really all that important, someday I will buy it back. If it is not that essential to my well being, then I won't miss it.

PEACE OF MIND

*I have learned the secret of being content in any and every situation,
whether well fed or hungry, whether living in plenty or want. I can
do everything through him who gives me strength.*

—Philippians 4: 12-13 NIV

Peace of mind can be found even in trying times. By learning to simplify our lives, we are better able to distinguish the difference between needs and wants. As our lifestyle becomes simpler, we can see priorities more clearly. When our minds are freed of superficial desires, we are more content and at peace within ourselves.

I once heard Christian author and financial expert, Larry Burkett, state these simple rules for living in contentment:

1. Live within your means.

2. Learn to give to others.

3. Establish priorities.

4. Be grateful for what you have.

5. Reject a fearful spirit.

Burkett often pointed out that there is a good reason the Bible often mentions money. There is nothing more apt to separate a man from God than his bank account. Money in itself is not the problem. It's over emphasizing the importance of money that causes difficulties. The lean times of unemployment remind us that security based on wealth can be fleeting. Only God holds the key to our security in the long run. He wants us to learn to depend on Him instead of our limited resources which can evaporate at any time.

DO'S AND DON'TS FOR THE UNEMPLOYED

There are no absolute rules for surviving unemployment. Although not everyone is faced with the same kinds of problems, there are suggestions commonly offered as a means of survival. The ones offered below are meant to stimulate your thinking about your choices.

Here are some things to avoid:

1. Don't assume you will only be out of work a short time.

2. Don't continue the use of credit cards if you can avoid it.

3. Don't buy non-essentials. Save cash for food, rent, child care, and the like.

4. Don't ignore loved ones. Keep lines of communication open with family members.

5. Don't wait too long before you apply for unemployment benefits. Apply as soon as you learn you are laid off.

6. Don't ignore your creditors. Let them know you plan to honor your commitments to them.

These suggestions may be helpful:

1. Do take time to budget income you receive before you begin spending. It will help to maintain your priorities.

2. Do get credit counseling if you are in a financial bind.

3. Do let friends and family members know of your need for work.

4. Do inventory all assets and consider selling non-essential items.

5. Do examine the job market and start networking with others in your career field.

6. Do maintain any insurance coverage you have if at all possible.

POWERLESSNESS

○ ○

Be anxious for nothing, but in everything by prayer and supplication with thanksgiving let your requests be known to God.

—Philippians 4:6 NAS

Nothing is apt to make us feel more powerless than being out of work for a lengthy period of time. We start feeling helpless in the face of overwhelming circumstances. What can we do to regain our sanity and peace of mind?

Acknowledging powerlessness over certain areas of our existence simply means we accept the fact that we do not have control over them. It could be people, events, or situations. When we accept our powerlessness, we give up trying to control what is not in our power to control. Recognizing our limitations helps us become more patient, flexible and sane.

GOD'S ANSWER

My God, my God, why hast thou forsaken me? Why art thou so far from helping me and the words of my roaring?

—Psalm 22:1 KJV

Jobless times are hard to endure. Like David in the Bible, we may feel God has forsaken us. Our prayer is usually that we be delivered from our struggles. We want the problem solved and done with right away. We say, "Lord, get me out of this mess." God's answer may be to give us the energy to deal with the problem and see it through to the end.

If we grow weary of waiting for an answer to our prayers, it might be helpful to ask some hard questions. Begin by asking, "What have I been doing with the answers God has been providing?" The second question should be, "Am I ready to accept the answer God has for me?" While these questions may make us uncomfortable, they can help us stay honest with ourselves and our God.

So what is God's answer to those who face unemployment? I believe He wants His people to be employed. It is from our labor that we are best able to serve Him and others. You can be certain of one thing as you go about your search for work: God has not forsaken your cause. He wants you to find suitable work to sustain your life. He wants to shower you with the blessings that are a product of your labor.

MOTIVATION

Have you noticed that motivation is seldom a problem when what you are doing is enjoyable? Perhaps that is why it is so hard to motivate yourself to look for work.

Most of us hate going out and making job contacts. Writing out job applications and resumes is hardly exciting. Unfortunately, employment experts tell us that searching for work is a full time job. Nothing less than an all-out effort will achieve the desired results. It's up to each of us to motivate ourselves in spite of the fact that we may dislike the task of job hunting.

Motivating yourself to look for work begins when you realize that searching for work is your main job. This means getting up in the morning and going out to sell yourself. While your faith and resolve will be constantly tested, you can count on the presence and support of God. He will supply the strength and courage necessary for daily tasks if you ask these things of Him. Don't forget to ask.

SLOW DAYS

Watch and pray so that you will not fall into temptation. The spirit is willing, but the body is weak.

—Matthew 26:41 NIV

Time passes so slowly some days. It's like nothing is happening and nothing is going to happen to change our condition of joblessness. What we fear most is this feeling of being at the end of our rope. During slow times it is easy to listen to the internal dialog of despair. The voice of depression always seems so convincing when we feel down and abandoned.

You must fight against the temptation to give in to discouragement. Go for a walk, re-examine your job hunt plan, or talk to a friend, but whatever you do, don't give in to your fears. Remember, there is at least as much reason for optimism as for despair in any situation. Keep praying. Keep working the disciplines of being responsible. But whatever you do, don't give up.

REJECTION

One of the most frustrating aspects of the job search is dealing with rejection. After being turned down time after time you want to give up and go home. Still, the best advice is to keep going. Make some additional employment calls, if possible. Always have a contingency plan so set backs don't get to you. Be positive and say to yourself, "At least I know the score at that place." If you recognize the fact that sorting out poor job prospects from good ones is one of your goals, then disappointment over being turned down will be considerably less.

Frequent rejection is hard on your self worth. You may start thinking there is no longer a place for you in the job world. Fight the temptation to get down on yourself. Remember there are lots of people out of work these days. Many employers are holding off hiring for fear the recovery may not be permanent. Still, in spite of continued worries about the economy, people are being hired theses days. Studies show that those who remain confident have a better chance of job hunting success. Keep telling yourself, "There is a job out there and it has my name on it."

PRAYER FOR A SLOW DAY

o o o o o o o o o o o o o o o o o o o o o o o o o o o o o o o o o

Give ear to my words, O Lord, consider my sighing. Listen to my cry for help, my King and my God, for to you I pray. In the morning, O Lord, you will hear my voice; in the morning I lay my requests before you and wait in expectation.

—Psalm 5: 1-3 NIV

Some days we start out at a crawl. It's hard to wake up and get going. Everything we do seems to be in slow motion. Everything seems difficult and disagreeable. We especially need sound habits of prayer and self discipline on slow days.

God, help me to get going. Help me to feel more enthusiastic. I would like to be a self-starter; someone who sees opportunity around every corner and finds hope in all things. Help me look to today and not to the past. Help me to see what a precious gift today is. Grant me a larger view that avoids being overly focused on the petty cares and concerns of life. Help me think of others' needs instead of just myself. Guard my tongue so I do not have to apologize for being inconsiderate today.

COPING WITH EMERGENCIES

o o o o o o o o o o o o o o o o o o o o o o o o o o o o o o

Sit loosely in the saddle of life.

—*Robert Louis Stevenson*

Most of us like our lives to be neat and tidy. One of the predicaments of the unemployed is that normal, daily problems have a way of becoming overwhelming. Everything seems like an emergency. Something on the car needs fixing, or the washing machine goes on the blink, or some other problem is in the making. It's easy to begin to panic. Anxiety about impending crises can keep you on edge and set you up for unending stress.

While being unemployed may be a major crisis, you do not need to develop an anxious mentality that rattles your nerves. Taking one thing at a time and living one day at a time helps alleviate a great deal of daily stress. Few things are so pressing that they can't wait a little while to be done. Slowing down a little can help you keep your priorities and thinking straight.

What things do you obsess about? Don't you get sick of twisting in the wind over things beyond your control? Maybe it's time to let go and let God handle them for a while.

MAKING YOUR OWN BED

One of the best indications that a person is exhibiting healthy self care is their commitment to sound habits which help maintain balance in their daily life.

—Author unknown

There are times when we don't feel like being very responsible. We get so tired of the job hunt and trying to do our best. This is when sound habits of daily living help keep you going. Being accountable to yourself, others, and God helps restore balance and gives purpose and meaning to life. It doesn't matter if you feel bright and chipper when you wake up in the morning. You need to get up and make the most of your day.

Carelessness about your daily life can lead to apathy and a lowering of personal standards. The cultivation of any habit that helps the day go more smoothly is well worth the effort. This inventory can help you add balance and stability to your daily life.

1. Try to get adequate rest at night.

2. Pray and meditate over the day at hand.

3. Eat a good breakfast.

4. Review yesterday's goals and set new objectives every day.

5. Establish your priorities for the coming hours.

6. Take time for personal grooming.

7. Do something you enjoy sometime during the day.

8. Exercise regularly.

THE IMPORTANCE OF
MAKING LISTS

o o o o o o o o o o o o o o o o o o o o o o o o o o o o o o o
There is a time for everything and a season for every activity under heaven.

—Ecclesiastes 3:1 NIV

Do not delude yourself into thinking that organization is no longer important now that you are unemployed. Quite the contrary. Making a list of each day's goals is an essential means of adding stability to life now that you lack the order of a job routine. The use of lists on a daily basis helps in setting goals, determining priorities, and staying on track with your objectives. One of the most important benefits of a daily list is that it gets you started for the day. Lists not only spark the engine of motivation, they are valuable road maps directing the course of your daily life. Without direction, you are apt to fall into patterns of self-defeating behavior.

Here are some basic rules for making and using lists effectively:

1. Lists are best written when there is time without disruptions.

2. Lists will be more useful if tasks are prioritized in their order of importance.

3. Lists should be kept where you can see them.

4. Review your list at the end of the day and set new goals for the coming day.

5. Use rewards with desirable incentives to help you complete difficult tasks.

6. Do the most difficult tasks first when your energy level is high

Today's reminder: Begin each day working on a list of goals. Morale and daily accomplishments will be much higher by evening.

FRUSTRATION

Many things are lost for want of asking.

—English Proverb

There are days when frustration about joblessness threatens to overwhelm us. Some times we don't know which way to turn. Society pushes the idea that everyone should be self-sufficient. How we hate admitting we are lost or at a dead end. It is especially difficult to acknowledge that we have lost our direction in life. Sitting and stewing only makes matters worse because we cannot think our way out of the dilemma.

It is often pride that keeps us stuck in the rut of despair. We simply don't have the right questions, let alone the right answers to our problem. When we get frustrated enough with the pain of our own indecisiveness, we may become more willing to accept help from others. Continued anger and paralysis are sure signs that we could use some new insights into our problems. There is nothing wrong with asking others for help. Everyone can benefit from wise counsel at some point in their life. Knowing when to let go and ask others to help us is a sign of wisdom and maturity.

INDECISIVENESS

Hear my cry, O God; listen to my prayer. From the ends of the earth I call to you, I call as my heart grows faint; lead me to the rock that is higher than I.

—Psalm 61: 1-2 NIV

Decisiveness is important in maintaining a sense of purpose and direction in life. Decisiveness contributes to a sense of confidence and general mental health. My own struggles with indecisiveness during periods of unemployment indicate that it has many roots. It sometimes stems from genuine tiredness and lack of energy. Often it is the result of unclear goals and priorities. Chronic indecision can also be symptomatic of deeper emotional confusion due to depression. Don't hesitate to seek professional help if you find it increasingly difficult to make decisions.

One of the best ways to fight indecisiveness is to make a conscious effort to pray throughout the day as you go about your job hunt. Ask God to show you what He would have you do with your life. Review daily goals frequently. Lists help keep track of your commitments and priorities. They can keep you from sliding off your objectives. Just remember a slip doesn't have to be a fall. You can get up and going again on your hunt to find a job.

DECISIVENESS

○ ○
When you know who you are, you will know what to do with your life.

—An old vocational education saying.

Being decisive can mean not acting, as well as acting to put our plans in motion. Many people would like to further their careers by returning to school, but they realize the price would be too high in terms of the disruption of their family relations. On the other hand, there are those who could finish an additional education program in the same amount of time it takes to decide to do something with their lives. We are apt to act decisively when we see ourselves clearly enough to know who we are and where we want to go with our life.

The main principles of sound decision making are having accurate information about yourself and a realistic understanding of your career options. Employment offices, college career counseling centers and local libraries can provide tools for self appraisal. Being well informed does not mean we will never make a mistake in choosing our course of action. It does indicate we can proceed with confidence as we consider factual information and prayerfully seek God's guidance. Once we have taken confident steps in the direction of our goal, indecisiveness is replaced by a renewed enthusiasm for completing our objective. The key to decisiveness is a willingness to act in our own behalf.

RE-EXAMINING A CAREER PATH

○ ○

You have got to know what it is you want, or someone is going to sell you a bill of goods somewhere along the line that can do irreparable damage to your self-esteem, your sense of worth and your stewardship of the talents that God gave you.

—*From "What Color is Your Parachute" by Richard Nelson Bolles*

When faced with unemployment you may need to re-examine your career path. Some career counselors recommend lining up options and examining them carefully. Do a thorough assessment of your present career. Begin with questions like: Does my career meet my interests, personality, abilities and aptitudes? If the answer is no, you may want to consider another area in the same field or a different career entirely.

Richard Nelson Bolles has written an excellent book on career assessment. His work, *What Color is Your Parachute?* suggests the following self evaluation.

1. Inventory skills and put them into categories.

2. Consider what skills you enjoy using the most.

3. Decide where you want to use your skills.

The key to successful self evaluation is a systematic approach to gathering information. Talk with peers in your field about their jobs, attend professional meetings and support groups, spend time at the library researching careers. Don't forget that local colleges and state agencies may have professional services which can assist you in your search. Seeking the help of someone experienced in career counseling is a wise choice. They have access to resources which can give you insight into the proper career for you.

ADVICE

Without consultation, plans are frustrated, But with many counselors they succeed.

—Proverbs 15:22 NAS

A boss of mine once told me, "Get all the advice you can and then do what you think is best for you." At first I thought his suggestion was flippant. But upon further reflection I realized he meant every word sincerely. Although advice may be cheap, it is one of the most valuable assets you can receive from others. For this reason it is wise to seek only the advice of those whose knowledge you respect.

Since God often works in our lives through others, we should never seek or take the advice of others too lightly. Remember, no one can make your career decisions for you. Only you can pay the price, in terms of time and energy expended, to maintain your choice. So, seek the best possible advice, consider the pros and cons of each choice, and then do what you think is best for you.

KEEP ON KEEPING ON

o o o o o o o o o o o o o o o o o o o o o o o o o o o o o o o o o o

This time like all times is a very good one if we know what to do with it.

—Ralph Waldo Emerson

Time moves slowly when you are out of work and that is why it's even more important to make "to do" lists. Working on lists can keep you from becoming overly preoccupied with whether you are going to get a phone call concerning the last job interview. I have found it helpful to imagine that I am going back to work in a few days. I ask myself, "Which things would I most like to get done?" Armed with a year's worth of rainy day jobs, I have even found myself hoping I don't get interrupted before some of the major items on my list are accomplished. Wouldn't you know, inevitably I have had to give up on completing some personal tasks because I needed to start back to work?

God, help me not to put off doing the things I need to do today. Remind me, no task is too big if I keep on doing the next thing in front of me.

UNEMPLOYMENT CHALLENGES YOUR VALUES

You cannot serve God and money. Therefore I tell you, do not worry about your life, what you will eat, or drink; or about your body, what you will wear. Is not life more important than food and the body more important than clothes?

—Matthew 6: 24-25 NIV

These words of Christ challenge us to reconsider our values. How strange they sound in our ears. We are so used to hearing the "get more, buy now" messages of our consumer culture that we sometimes forget his warning.

Times of unemployment forced me to examine my values as well as my priorities. I learned that sharing a cup of coffee with friends, going to the park with my kids, or just working in the yard could add as much enjoyment to daily life as more costly activities. The urge to get and spend eventually tapered off.

It's surprising how the mind comes to accept new realities of joblessness. The simple life is not that terrible after all. You will come to understand that your contentment need not depend on your ability to spend money. While going to the store without giving it a second thought is a hard habit to break, the withdrawal pains are not fatal. As your focus shifts to simpler activities, you find a real sense of peace. You learn that feeling needy often has as much to do with your frame of mind as your bank account.

WANTS VS. NEEDS

○ ○

Why spend money for what is not bread, and your labor on what does not satisfy?

—Isaiah 55: 2 NIV

Tough times call for tough choices. A period of unemployment makes us realize the difference between wants and needs. It forces us to think through even simple purchases. Many of the things we once thought were important aren't essential after all. Here are some things you may find unnecessary during unemployment. You are welcome to make your own list:

1. Shopping just to go shopping

2. Oil changes every 3000 miles

3. Movies or video rentals

4. Vacations

5. Cigarettes and alcohol

6. Junk food

7. Dry cleaning

8. Eating out

9. Unnecessary errands

10. Magazine subscriptions

11. Unnecessary long distance phone calls

12. Cable T.V.

IMPULSE BUYING

Self respect is the fruit of self discipline; the sense of dignity grows with the ability to say no to oneself.

—Abraham Heschel

The habit of spending money without much thought is deeply ingrained in most of us. This note in one of my journals reminds me just how hard it is to live within a strict budget day after day; week after week.

"Today I feel bad because I spent five dollars we needed for something else. I find it hard to accept the constraints of our budget. I honestly intended to live within my means for the week, yet suddenly I was tempted to buy some materials for a long-standing, but non-essential job around the house. I knew better but there I was, shelling out the money. I must be careful in the future to guard against those hidden imperatives that tell me certain jobs must be done right now. Perhaps it would help to review my budget more frequently. Next time I will be more alert to the dangers of impulse buying. Ah, the world is a dangerous place."

CONFUSION

○ ○

Live in the solution, not the problem.

—An Alcoholics Anonymous slogan

Some days we have the "I don't know's." We don't know what we want to do. We don't know what's going to happen or even where to start looking for a job. Uncertainty reigns in our life. When we are at the end of our mental resources it may indicate that we are stuck because we are seeking the wrong answers to our problem. If we are out of options it could be because we have become too selective in our search for work.

Being continually stymied in the job hunt may say more about our state of mind than our state of employment. We must keep coming back to the fact that we need to be working. The decision we must sometimes make is, "Am I willing to take whatever job is available in order to find work?" If we focus on the decision that needs to be made rather than the problem, the solution may soon appear.

WITHDRAWAL

He who is out the front door already has a good part of his journey behind him.

—Dutch Proverb

There is a tendency to avoid social interaction when you are unemployed. It is not easy to talk to others when you are preoccupied with your own problems. While it is impossible to avoid some of the negative feelings associated with being out of work, you don't have to give in to these depressing side effects. Remember it's your choice.

You must fight the urge to withdraw from society because you are out of work. By forcing yourself to go out and meet the public you are encouraged to become more interested in others and their lives. It gets your mind off yourself. You might just hear some new job leads by letting others know of your condition. As someone has said, "Loneliness is as much a problem of insulation as isolation." You cannot afford to indulge in self-isolating behavior. Stay involved with your family and society at large. It is the best way to keep connected to reality and the world of work.

SUPPORT SYSTEMS

No man is an island.

—*John Donne*

I once read of an auto worker who had endured many long layoffs in the course of his career. When asked how he survived what must have been many months of bitter disappointment, he answered by saying, "I could never have endured those times without the support of my wife and my church."

It sounds too simple, doesn't it? Yet every person needs a support system to help deal with a major crisis. For some, the caring support comes from friends and family. For others it may be a church pastor, support group, or vocational counselor. No matter what resources you use, it's important to keep in touch with them on a regular basis. No one, no matter how strong, is free of the need for encouragement and understanding. Remember, you do not need to go through this jobless time alone.

A sound support system should include:

1. People you can trust with your feelings

2. People who understand your situation and are willing to take time to listen to you

3. People with whom you have easy and regular access

4. People who are healthy, positive role models and are willing to be honest with you.

DEPRESSION

Why are you downcast, O my soul? Why are you so disturbed within me? Put your hope in God, for I will yet praise him, my Savior and my God.

—Psalm 42:11 NIV

Depression is sneaky. It often comes upon us without our being fully aware of what is happening. We get depressed when looking back at the past weeks of unemployment and asking what we have accomplished. We feel discouraged about the uncertainty of the future. We may even blame ourselves for getting into our present state of joblessness. All these exercises in futility are sure fire guarantees for producing despondency. They create within us an atmosphere of melancholy and despair.

Sometimes we are unable to shake the blues. If feelings of grief and depression persist week after week, take action. Counseling can help us regain balance and rebuild self worth. Almost everyone can benefit from some form of wise counsel at some point in their life. Counseling is about searching for the best possible solution. It enables us to gain new perspectives on our problems. Often we learn we have more choices than we had previously thought. Staying stuck and confused only perpetuates inertia and contributes to an ongoing state of depression. One of the best remedies for depression is to create a new plan of action for the kind of life we want for ourselves.

Any form of depression should be taken seriously. If you are suffering from the long term effects of depression, you may need to seek medical help. There is nothing wrong with getting medical assistance for problems that interfere with your health.

SELF ESTEEM

For you created my inmost being; you knit me together in my mother's womb. I praise you because I am fearfully and wonderfully made; your works are wonderful. I know that full well.

—*Psalm 139:13-14 NIV*

The Bible tells us that each human being is a special creation of God. Sometimes we forget that we are special people in God's eyes. Sooner or later being out of work is bound to affect our self esteem. It's difficult to feel good about yourself when your life is on hold. When your self worth is low, you may become more critical of yourself and others. Your morale goes down hill and motivation to search for work suffers.

It's hard work to keep a positive attitude about yourself when you are unemployed. Here are a few suggestions to help avoid the temptation of negative self criticism:

1. Remind yourself that as one of God's people you are inferior to no one.

2. Write out all your positive traits and skills and review them often.

3. Continue to maintain your personal appearance.

4. Volunteer some time to help others.

5. Take care of yourself by getting enough rest and eating right.

6. Stay in touch with positive people who make you feel good about yourself.

7. Guard your internal dialog against negative self talk.

8. Continue to practice your faith and live up to your values.

LIFE HAS MEANING IN SPITE OF BEING JOBLESS

A sure way for one to lift himself up is by helping lift someone else.

—Booker T. Washington

The longer you are unemployed the more you are apt to feel devalued. You may even start to believe your life has become meaningless. This negative, one-sided point of view is self-destructive. Human beings create meaning through their actions. When you are barred from normal productive activities, there is a need to find other outlets for your energy. You may have to substitute volunteer work or other forms of creative endeavor, but you can create new purpose and meaning for your life.

Volunteering can sometimes lead to a permanent full time job. It never hurts your resume to show that your care about helping others. If nothing else, it can help make your community a better place. You get to meet new people and make new friends. Volunteers often gain new skills and knowledge which can later be useful in other lines of work. A final reason to volunteer is to get out of yourself. You naturally feel better when helping others whose needs are greater than your own.

SELF RENEWAL

One ought, each day at least, hear a little song, read a good poem, see a fine picture, and if possible speak a few reasonable words.

—Goethe

Many years ago I was unemployed in a large western city. It was during a recession and I was having a tough time finding any work. I used to job hunt in the mornings and then take a break in the afternoons to stop at the museum of fine art. I don't know if my leave of absence from the job search hindered my chances for employment in any way. I do know that to this day I have never regretted having enjoyed the great art treasures of that city. It was just the boost my sagging morale needed during those tough times.

Just because you are unemployed doesn't mean you do not deserve to occasionally take some time for yourself. Now and then a visit to an art gallery, park, museum or library may be just what you need to reawaken an interest in other things besides the job search. Nurturing your mind and soul is never wasted time. Any activity which can refresh and give new meaning to life may ultimately pay higher dividends for your mental and spiritual health. Such activities can reawaken the creative urge to take an active part in choosing the course your life will take.

OUR TALENTS

We have different gifts according to the grace given us.

—Romans 12:6 NIV

The Bible tells us that God has given each person certain gifts. These gifts are reflected in one way or another in our careers. Unfortunately, when we are unable to use our talents, we may become bitter and contemptuous of our God-given gifts. In a job market that does not have an immediate place for us, we may be tempted to believe our skills are worthless. This is self-destructive thinking.

We must fight this temptation to devalue our abilities. True, we may not be able to find work in our chosen area, but that does not mean we cannot build on our existing skills. In time we may even be able to develop a new and more useful career from the foundation of our talents and skills.

Remember, careers which are man made, may come and go, but our talents, which come from God, will serve us well throughout our life.

INNER RESOURCES

○ ○

It's autumn,
and in my hut
nothing,
yet everything.

—*Author Unknown*

The author of this Haiku poem reminds us that we have within us many of the essential ingredients to sustain our lives. This is not to say we are totally self-sufficient. It does mean that we have the resilience and tenacity as human beings to live with very little dependence on the outside world. It is reassuring to realize that we can survive with very few material things. We know we can go on even in jobless times when our finances are slim.

There are many different kinds of inner resources. Some that come to mind are the ability to pray, meditate and fast. Industriousness, ingenuity and steadfastness could also be included. What are some of your inner resources? Ask someone who knows you to help you name some. It will be good for your morale to become more aware of the personal strengths of your character that others see in you.

DIGNITY

Sometimes the people you ask for work may be abrupt. It's like they don't want to give you the time of day. Let's face it. There are many more horses' rears in the world than horses. You are bound to run into one of them now and then. When you do, remind yourself, you need not lose your dignity just because you are presently out of work. You have the right to the respect of others. You have the right to be proud of your work skills and to become your own advocate in trying to sell those skills.

It's important to keep these points in mind when seeking work. If there is dignity in labor, then there is certainly dignity in seeking to find work. Work is the inalienable right of everyone in a free society and everyone's responsibility. Without the opportunity to seek and find one's work in life, freedom is a hollow illusion. No one should ever look down on you for seeking work. So go on with your search, knowing you have every right to feel proud of your effort to find steady employment.

HUMOR IS ESSENTIAL

o o o o o o o o o o o o o o o o o o o o o o o o o o o o o o o o o o o
The best thing about the future is that it comes only one day at a time.

—*Abraham Lincoln*

Someone once jokingly suggested I call my book, *The Enjoyment of Unemployment.* Unfortunately, there isn't much humor to be found in being out of a job. I know. There is just too much anxiety and worry involved. While being unemployed is no laughing matter, one can profit by keeping his sense of humor intact during hard times. Humor helps reduce stress and keeps us from taking ourselves too seriously. We might say laughter helps lubricate the wheels of endurance. A good laugh now and then nourishes fortitude and makes it easier to cope with life's trials.

Laughter is nature's way of helping our body relax. A relaxed person who can still find something to laugh about is likely to make a better impression in job interviews than one who is filled with gloom and doom. Do your best to keep and cultivate a sense of humor. Read the comics. Take in a funny movie now and then, if possible. Above all else, stay in touch with positive people who laugh a lot. It will do you and your job hunt a world of good.

THE LONG TERM VIEW

o o o o o o o o o o o o o o o o o o o o o o o o o o o o o o o o o

But I trust in you, O Lord; I say, "You are my God." My times are in your hands…

—Psalm 31: 14-15 NIV

The philosophy of living one day at a time has much to commend it. There are times when the present twenty-four hours are all you can handle. Still, living a day at a time does not mean you cannot benefit from occasionally taking a long term view. In spite of setbacks, you have the potential to make the coming years the best ones of your life. Look at the example of Buckminster Fuller. At a low point in his career, he almost gave up on living all together. In later years, he was to become world famous for his work on the architecture of geodesic domes.

Time and again, personal life histories teach that no one can predict the outcome of any given time span. If you look back over the past decade, could you honestly have imagined all you have accomplished? So it is with the next period. There are undreamed achievements and experiences waiting for you. Don't sell your life short before you have lived it. Remember, your times are in God's hands. He will not let you down, if you seek His will for your life.

LIFE WORK

When the specter of unemployment frightens us, it's easy to forget that lifework is more than what you can get paid for.

—Jennifer James—from the book
"Success is the Quality of Your Journey"

Jennifer James has written widely about life and the many ways we can enhance its quality. She believes that life work is a broad term which applies to more than simply how we make our living. Life work encompasses mental and spiritual growth as well as our career development. It includes many changes throughout our life span. In essence, our life work determines who we are and what we become as human beings.

When the crisis of unemployment threatens your security, it is easy to forget that your life work is more than just a job. Life work, in the broadest sense, is also commitment to family relationships, to friends, and to God. The richness of life depends on many things. If you choose, you can continue much of your life work while going about the business of looking for steady employment. By continuing regular social routines and staying connected with friends, family, and community, you are still able to keep many crucial aspects of your life work intact.

LOOK UP—BE LIFTED UP

I lift up my eyes to you whose throne is in heaven.

—*Psalm 123:1 NIV*

Many years ago my family and I attended a small church in a rural community in the Midwest. It was in the dead of winter and the services were being held in the back of the sanctuary in order to save on heating costs. As my eyes surveyed the unfamiliar surroundings, they were drawn upward toward the large stained glass windows. What I still remember most is a small plaque above the highest pane. The tiny letters on it read: "Look up. Be lifted up." It was a welcome message that I was much in need of in those days, for I was faced with much job uncertainty.

When you are unemployed, it is easy to start looking down. You may feel pressured by overwhelming needs. The cost of living goes on while the cash flow has stopped or become extremely limited. No wonder your attitude becomes more somber with each passing day.

Turning your eyes away from your immediate problems is difficult. Yet scripture reminds us that our God is the God of hope and renewal. The act of raising our eyes to Him elevates our spirit. Something different happens to the way we view ourselves and our problems when we look upward to Him. We become more calm, patient, and filled with hope in His presence.

SUCCESS

o o o o o o o o o o o o o o o o o o o o o o o o o o o o o o o o o o o o o

There are many kinds of success worth having.

—*Theodore Roosevelt*

Success in terms of the human ego usually means obtaining wealth, status or security of some kind. Success in the spiritual sense is oriented toward God's will for us. What is spiritual success? Peace, harmony, giving, sharing, forgiving, listening, nurturing, self-forgetting, gratitude, and humility. Have you been successful today? Have you reached the point in your life when you can focus attention on spiritual as well as material success? What is it that you really need in life? Does your present life reflect what's really important?

It is interesting to pose this question occasionally, especially at the end of a long, fruitless day of job hunting. Was I spiritually successful today? You can answer yes if you can say you have worked hard at your search for work, stayed out of self pity, and been honest with and considerate of others. You have the right to feel good about many achievements in your life even if you are unemployed. Success is staying with the job hunt when you would rather give up. Success is being kind to others when you don't feel very good about your life. Success is living within your budget. It's making it through another day. Don't forget to note all your successes today. They are more important than you think.

REMEMBERING PAST SUCCESSES

Why are you downcast, O my soul? Why are you so disturbed within me? Put your hope in God for I will yet praise him, my Savior and my God.

—Psalm 42: 11 NIV

Psalm 42 finds David questioning why he has become so discouraged. The answer comes when he is reminded that God is still in charge. In Psalm 44, David is comforted by the memory of God's past victories over his people's enemies.

You can also benefit from David's example. When you are down on your luck, you feel like the whole world is out to get you. It really isn't, you know. It just feels that way. It's the voice of depression and despair talking. Don't give in to negative feelings and thoughts. Fight the temptation to interpret everything that is happening in your life as a personal attack. Remind yourself that God is still in control of major outcomes in today's world. Recall all the things of the past that have gone right in your life. You can start over. The sun will shine again. You'll see.

I MEANT IT FOR GOOD

○ ○

And we know that all things work together for the good of them who love God, to them who are called according to his purpose.

—Romans 8:28 KIV

Being unemployed is more than a separate, unrelated incident in your career. It is an integral part of the search for who you are and where you are going in life. It involves not only your journey into the outside world in search of work, but also your inner journey in search of who you wish to become. If you are patient and persevere in your search, you may find rewards far beyond your expectations.

While it is painful to have your life so drastically changed, the crisis of unemployment can present you with valuable opportunities for both career and personal development. Those who have suffered radical change in their lives frequently report that while it was painful at the time, much good came about as a result of the transition. President Jimmy Carter lost his bid for a second term in office, yet now is recognized for his humanitarian efforts. He could have become bitter and withdrawn from public life. Instead he kept on doing what he felt God had called him to do. In the end, the former President has achieved even greater acclaim than when he was in office.

LAZINESS VS. TIREDNESS

o o o o o o o o o o o o o o o o o o o o o o o o o o o o o o o o o

Do not love sleep or you will grow poor; stay awake and you will have food to spare.

—Proverbs 20:13 NIV

It's tough to get going on days when you feel apathetic and lethargic. It's at times like this that you especially need lists. You may not be very effective on hang down days, but you will feel better when evening comes if you keep working on your goals.

Anxiety and worry over joblessness can cause sleeplessness and physical discomfort. So don't be afraid to baby yourself occasionally. Take a hot bath and a short nap, then get back to work on your search for work. Whatever you do, don't give up on your objectives. Keep plugging along, one step at a time and one task at a time. Reward yourself when you are through with a difficult job, preferably not with food. Take a walk, listen to music, read something inspirational. The main thing is to keep your equilibrium and momentum by continuing to work on your goals.

Prayer for Today

God, I feel so drug out today. I don't know how I can wake up so tired some days. At times like these, help me to know that anything I accomplish is better than nothing. Help me to know that conditions in my life do not have to be ideal in order for me to make real progress in my search for work. Thank you, Lord, for restoring my faith, hope and strength when they are low.

LIMITED OPTIONS

For God did not give us a spirit of timidity, but a spirit of power, of love and of self discipline.

—*II Timothy 1: 7 NIV*

It may seem that the longer you are unemployed, the fewer choices you have. The nature of the present economy in America is that many job possibilities are no longer available. Still, opportunities do exist. The question is, "What can I do to get back to work?" Perhaps it's time to consider your remaining choices. Should you consider moving to a different geographic area in order to find work? What about returning to school? Would it be best to take any job and keep looking for work in your preferred field?

You don't have to make a decision right away. Take some time today to write out the options that are now available to you. List and weigh the pros and cons of each possible choice. Given your present circumstances, you should be able to see more clearly what works best for you. Don't hesitate in asking for the advice of others. Receiving the right information at the right time often proves to be invaluable.

Even if your job choices are limited these days, you can still make head way toward important goals. The decisions you make today can move you closer to a brighter future.

PROCRASTINATION

o o o o o o o o o o o o o o o o o o o o o o o o o o o o o o o o

Procrastination is a thief of time.

—Edward Young

Procrastination is a major obstacle for the unemployed person. Putting things off is often the result of feelings of powerlessness. When you feel hopeless about your destiny, you may give up on trying to do your best. By giving in to negative emotions and thoughts, the positive forces of self confidence and hope are neutralized. In their place come the paralyzing influences of self pity and discouragement. The more you focus on fears and worries, the more immobilized you are apt to become in the vicious cycle of procrastination.

I admit it. I'm a terrible procrastinator. I have discovered that the reason I tend to put things off is that I don't really think I will have to pay a price for it. How is that for denial? But I have found a solution. I single out one task, and I tell myself it is the only thing I will focus on until it gets done. It's aggravating to have to give up other diversions, but no excuses can be allowed. In order to deal with the problem, I find it helpful to narrow down my list of priorities. By establishing what comes first, I'm able to stay focused on the main task until it's completed.

It takes special effort to break out of this rut of procrastination. We must go to war against its inertia. Starting new habits of exercise, joining a support group and getting counseling are just a few ways to break out of the trap of procrastination. The key to success is to get started on a new path and stay with it. Taking one step at a time one day at a time will help break down resistance to action.

ON KEEPING FIT

○ ○

*No temptation has seized you except what is common to man. And
God is faithful; He will not let you be tempted beyond what you can
bear. But when you are tempted, He will also provide a way out so
you can stand up under it.*

—I Corinthians 10:13 NIV

The major problem we face during unemployment is having too much unstruc-
tured time on our hands. When we are idle, apathy and laziness tend to grow.
There is great danger of dissipating our energies on non-productive activities.
Spending too much time in front of the television or the refrigerator are examples
of dangerous forms of escapism. It takes real self discipline to set limits on personal appetites.

Saying you will not watch T.V. past a certain hour or eat between meals is
hard. But unless you maintain healthy living habits, unhealthy ones may take up
residency in your life.

Some of the disciplines I have found useful in maintaining mental, physical
and spiritual health are:

1. Reading Scripture and other inspirational literature to begin each day.

2. Associating with positive people of faith

3. Practicing daily prayer and meditation

4. Exercising regularly by walking or other activities.

5. Keeping a journal and writing down my thoughts each day

6. Writing out daily to do lists and establishing priorities.

JOB HUNTING BURN OUT

How refreshing the whinny of a packhorse unloaded of everything.

—*Zen saying*

One of the hardest tasks you will ever undertake is looking for work. It is perhaps the most demanding and frustrating experiences a person can face. Being under the gun, trying to stay positive, and being upbeat for job interviews is physically and emotionally exhausting.

You may not be involved in the job search a full eight hours every day, but the pursuit of work is never far from your mind. Such ongoing stress is bound to take its toll. While it may seem ludicrous to speak of job search burn out, those of us who have looked for work day after day, week after week, know it's a reality. In order to fight burn out, plan each day's activities wisely. Use your most energetic part of the day for face to face contacts with prospective employers when possible. Save paper work for when you are still able to focus on such items without being overly tired.

In addition to pacing yourself on the daily job search, you may want to take a break from the routine now and then. Even if you can only get away for a day, try to take time for self renewal. You will look better, feel better, and be more optimistic when you come back to the job hunt.

FORTITUDE

○ ○
Be strong and take heart, all you who hope in the Lord.

—Psalm 31: 24 NIV

Years ago I worked as a high school counselor on a Native American reservation. I learned that native people have incorporated the idea of fortitude deep into their value system. Fortitude, to them, means being able to bear life's hardships without complaining. They have learned that bellyaching only makes matters difficult to bear and demoralizes everyone, including the complainer. The habit of griping about petty cares can affect your entire outlook on life. Soon the mountains and the mole hills all start appearing the same.

Constant complaining about being out of a job is apt to hinder your progress in finding work. Instead of accepting the situation as it is and moving on, you only intensify your misery by dwelling on problems. Do your best today to get rid of your list of woes. Try hard to practice fortitude, and avoid weighing yourself and others down with self-defeating talk that begins with 'if only.', 'I could have.', or 'they should have…'

WAITING FOR GOD'S GUIDANCE

Be still before the Lord and wait patiently for him

—Psalm 37:7 NIV

A Quaker friend of mine often speaks of asking God for a "leading" before making serious decisions. I once asked her what she did when there was no clear directive coming from above. She said, "That usually means I wait before taking further action." Waiting for God's leading in our lives can be difficult at times, but it is always the wisest choice. Waiting provides time to gather more information about our options. It also gives us a chance to consider input from family members and friends.

Taking time to pray and meditate over decisions needs to be an important part of your spiritual life. The Bible is filled with stories of people who paid a heavy price because they were in too great a hurry to wait for God's guidance. One example is the early Hebrew people. They spent forty years wandering in the wilderness because of their headstrong, impatient ways. They failed to realize they could not force their timing on God's plan for their lives.

There are some positive things you can do while waiting for God's answers in your job search. Do more research to gain new insights. Consult others for their advice and plan for the future. Keep praying for the wisdom and courage to accept God's answers when they do come. Sometimes being patient is your most important job.

PERSEVERANCE

o o o o o o o o o o o o o o o o o o o o o o o o o o o o o o o o o

And we rejoice in the hope of the glory of God. Not only so, but we rejoice in our sufferings, because we know that suffering produces perseverance, perseverance, character, and character, hope.

—Romans 5: 2-4 NIV

It was a foggy, winter, California morning some years ago. The chilly air matched the reception I got when I applied for work at a small convenience store. The manager looked me up and down with a skeptical eye. Then he said, "Son, this is January and this is the San Joaquin Valley. I wouldn't give you a plug nickle for your chances of finding a job today." On that discouraging note I left the shop thinking "Thanks for nothing, Mister." Fortunately, I did not give up my search for work. Before the day was out, I had a job.

I learned two valuable lessens from that experience. First, no one can predict your chances of finding employment. Secondly, persistence is the key that unlocks the door to finding a job. It's the only key that is guaranteed to work in the long run.

Impatience and despair are the two biggest enemies of an unemployed person. After a while you may begin to despair of another meaningless foray into a cold, heartless world that doesn't seem to need you. It takes real courage to keep going out and looking for work each day. Simply trust that your perseverance will eventually win out.

Searching for work is something only you can do for yourself, but you don't have to do it entirely alone. If you are getting to the end of your own resources, ask others for their input. Brainstorm. Go over the contacts you have already made. Maybe there is someone you can recontact. Examine the Yellow Pages for additional job possibilities. Perhaps there is an option you have overlooked. Keep searching, and pray while you search. Whatever you do, don't give up. Some days it's all you can do to make one legitimate job contact, so don't get discouraged. The law of averages favors the success of those who keep trying.

HOW LONG WILL I HAVE TO ENDURE?

○ ○

And we know that God causes all things to work together for the good of those who love God, to those who are called according to his purpose.

—Romans 8:28 NAS

The longer you are unemployed, the more you are tempted ask, "How long must I suffer this seemingly endless search for work?" Of course, there is no definite answer because the solution is not entirely in your hands. All you can know for certain is that your job hunt will take as long as it takes. How then are you to cope with the seeming endlessness of the job search?

If you believe that nothing happens here on earth without God's knowledge or concern, then being between jobs is not simply a meaningless experience to be endured. To a person of faith, the question is not merely, "How long must I wait for work?" but "How shall I live in the mean time?"

The hopeless person is just waiting for something to happen while the proactive person of faith asks, "How can this time best be used and how would God have me use it?" Today, pray for the renewal of your faith and the wisdom to use your time constructively. God promises to renew your strength and guide you when you trust in Him and strive to fit into His plan.

FAITH

○ ○

Faith is: Confidence in God's faithfulness to me in an uncertain world—on an uncharted course, toward an unknown future.

—Pamela Reeve, from the book "Faith Is"

Living completely by faith is one condition most people try to avoid at all costs. It's hard to live by faith, but ironically, when it comes right down to it, that's all that gets us through tough times. Just plain, stubborn faith that keeps us plodding along and doing the next thing in front of us.

Where does this faith to keep going come from? I believe faith is God's gift to those who keep praying and trying, in spite of what life has dished out. Faith means surrendering our will to God. By turning our lives over to the care of God, we discover the courage and strength necessary to meet life's challenges.

Faith is more than an abstract term. It takes real faith to continue the job search day after day. It takes faith to fill out one more job application when you feel the effort is fruitless. Real faith is courage in action. When you step out in faith, God steps in to help you by renewing your strength and courage for another day.

DISAPPOINTMENT

How long, O Lord, will you forget me forever? How long will you hide your face from me? How long must I wrestle with my thoughts and every day have sorrow in my heart?

—Psalm 13: 1 NIV

There is a certain sadness that comes when hope for a particular job fades. You have tried to do all that you could to make the job come through. You have made the contact, sent out your resume, filled out the job application, and prayed. Still, nothing happens. Slowly you realize that another job opportunity has evaded you. Was it the luck of the draw, or did you leave something out? Is there anything you might have done to have enhanced your position? If you are really curious, you can re-contact the employer and ask input on ways you might have presented yourself more successfully. If you don't wish to belabor the matter, the best thing to do is to feel happy for the person who got the job. He or she probably needed it as much as you did. Consider the possibility that something more suitable will eventually come along. The important thing to remember is not to take failure to land a particular job personally. Keep trusting that God has something in mind for you. His timing is never wrong. He will not let you down.

HONESTY

o o o o o o o o o o o o o o o o o o o o o o o o o o o o o o o o o o o

Do not let kindness and truth leave you. Bind them around your neck. Write them on the tablet of your heart.

—Proverbs 3: 3 NAS

There are many definitions of honesty. Basically, it boils down to willingness to tell the truth in our dealings with others. Being open and honest about your intentions when you are applying for work is not always easy. You want to appear positive and self confident, but secretly you may doubt whether the job is the right fit. You do have the right to ask the employer about the nature of the job and his expectations of his employees. If you seriously doubt that you are qualified for the job, it's alright to say so right at the start. On the other hand, you may wish to give the job a try to see if you can handle it.

One of the keys to honest thinking is a thorough understanding of your own skills, values and interests. Self awareness is the best way to determine where you want to go with your career life. Self awareness alone cannot make you honest. Only God can help you achieve this end. Trust that God will show you what job is best if you strive to be honest and transparent with others. It can be scary to leave the results of your job hunt in God's hands. That is why you need to pray for the willingness to be willing every day as you search for work.

DISHONESTY

If you tell the truth, you have infinite power supporting you; but if you do not, you have infinite power against you.

—*Charles Gordon*

Every job hunter has days when he or she is tempted to throw in the towel and go home early. It's no wonder. When the job possibilities seem less than appetizing, it's hard to feel enthusiastic about limited choices. "What's the use?"we ask ourselves, "There is nothing out there for me." Unfortunately, there is a price to be paid for this kind of defeatist thinking. It is found in a lowering of self worth and lost job opportunities.

The jobless person must constantly struggle with issues of dishonesty and integrity. At the end of the day we have either looked for work or we have not. Deep inside, we know whether our search has been enthusiastic or half hearted. Honesty and sincerity are two standards on which we must base our daily job search if we are to be effective. It is scary to put our integrity on the line each time we go out looking for work, but being in touch with God's plan for us requires nothing less. Reading God's word and praying for His guidance can help us stay honest with ourselves and others. They are excellent ways to begin preparing for each day's search for work.

WHAT DO YOU VALUE MOST?

o o o o o o o o o o o o o o o o o o o o o o o o o o o o o o o o o

The cost of a thing is the amount of what I will call life which is required to be exchanged for it, immediately or in the long run.

—H. D Thoreau

I once read about an actor who gave up a promising acting role in Hollywood in order to be with his family in New York. He was not willing to sacrifice his values to further his career. Unfortunately, that would not have been a common decision for many of us. Often we are tempted to make career choices which are destructive of our relationships with others. Are we willing to sacrifice our serenity, our family relationships, or even our religious convictions for the money or the status found in a particular job? Certainly we need to meet the economic necessities of life. But we also need to think seriously about the long term consequences of our career decisions.

1. Is the work something I would really enjoy doing?

2. How will the work affect my relationship with my family?

3. Is the work in keeping with my values?

4. How will the job affect my mental and physical health?

5. How far will I have to commute to my work place?

These are important questions for anyone in search of a job. They may not be easy questions but, they are essential ones involving the direction of our lives and the quality of our personal relationships with God and those persons closest to us.

CHOICES

When you have to make a choice and you don't make it, that is in itself a choice.

—*William James*

Our deepest depression frequently comes upon us when we refuse to accept responsibility for our own life. As long as we are willing to utilize our own choices we can feel pretty good about ourselves. It's when we try to run away from the responsibility to act in our own behalf that we start hating life. Sometimes we deceive ourselves by taking too much time to make up our minds. It's known as analysis paralysis. Refusing to choose keeps us locked in a cycle of inertia and despair. We are like a person standing at the end of a diving board looking down at the water. It's the tenth time we have climbed up there but we just can't bring ourselves to jump.

Staying immobilized is demoralizing but, we need not stay stuck. The way out is found in action. When we exercise our freedom to choose and act, we create meaning and purpose in our life. Our ability to act decisively gives us creative choices. It helps us gain control of our life and our destiny. Taking action does not always guarantee we will make the right choice. Still, a prudent decision made after careful deliberation is more likely to help us succeed than staying stuck in analysis paralysis.

INSINCERITY

The most exhausting thing in life is being insincere.

—Ann Morrow Lindbergh

Every out-of-work person who draws unemployment benefits soon learns there are two jobs. The first task is finding steady, suitable employment. The second is finding legitimate job contacts each week in order to keep the unemployment checks coming in regularly. The problem is that the longer a person is out of work, the fewer suitable job possibilities remain. When this happens, it is tempting to pad the weekly record with contacts of employers for whom we really don't wish to work.

There are no easy solutions to this double bind. I know what it's like. I've struggled with the problem myself, and always hated it. We may wish to be honest, but we dare not risk losing our unemployment check. The best advice is to plan your contacts wisely, be honest, and keep going back to those employers whose needs fit your job skills. A word to the wise. Careful scheduling of weekly job contacts can help prevent the need for questionable tactics later.

SOUL SEARCHING

o o o o o o o o o o o o o o o o o o o o o o o o o o o o o o o o o o o o o

Whoever loves money never has money enough; whoever loves wealth
is not satisfied with his income. This too is meaningless.

—Ecclesiastes 5:10 NIV

Good economic times have frequently encouraged job hopping. In fact, those who want to fast track their careers have been encouraged to switch employers frequently. Getting ahead in America today seems to be more about gaining money and prestige than maintaining loyalty and commitment to a higher set of values. Unfortunately, jumping from one job to the next can backfire. We never learn the value of being loyal to anyone but ourselves.

Working without any sense commitment creates a narrow world view. We may not take time to look very deeply into ourselves or the most critical issues of life like: Why am I here? Where am I going? What is my purpose in life?

While being unemployed is uncomfortable, it can provide the slowdown we need to do some serious soul searching. It gives us a fresh opportunity to examine where we want to go with our life. The importance of this time may seem meager compared to a steady pay check Still being grounded in a deeper sense of purpose can lead to a far richer, more meaningful life in the long run.

GOD IS STILL IN CHARGE

They have rights that dare to defend them.

—Roger Baldwin

You may ask, what good is faith and prayer if my job has been off-shored and no longer exists? It's a fair question. I believe God is still in charge. He still demands justice for his people. This does not mean you should sit idly by and accept national and local policies that erode your rights as a worker.

What can you do when faced with government and business practices that undermine your rights and welfare? Here are a few suggestions that might help:

First, know your rights. A good place to begin informing yourself is the 1986 Catholic Church proclamation, *Economic Justice for All.* It reminds us that a just society has a moral obligation to uphold and defend the rights of its workers. The economy exists for the person and not the person for the economy.

Second, become more politically active. Learn where your elected officials stand on key issues and contact them with your concerns.

Third, enlist the moral authority of church leaders in your community to support fair labor laws and practices. The *Job Loss Guide for Pastors,* published by the North Carolina Council of Churches, is an excellent example of what religious and civic leaders can do.

Finally, become involved in organizations such as unions to address your concerns and issues. Solidarity is the key to meeting the challenges of the global economy. Workers in the United States must join together with those of other countries to defend their right to a living wage. All who do the work have a right to be treated with dignity and respect.

HOPE FOR THE FUTURE

"For I know the plans I have for you," declares the Lord, "plans to prosper you and not to harm you, plans to give you a hope and a future. Then you will call upon me, and I will listen to you. You will seek me and find me when you seek me with all your heart."

—Jeremiah 29: 11-12 NIV

The Bible tells us of God's faithfulness to his people throughout time. He wants to give us a hope and a future. His Word calls out to us today, just as it did to the Hebrew people of the past. Its message is one of comfort and encouragement. It tells of God's desire for a relationship with us. He promises to renew the hope of those who sincerely accept His lordship over their life.

Most of us carry with us in our hearts a vision of our hopes and dreams for the future. Over the years we may have been forced to reassess that vision in light of new realities. When faced with a major set back like unemployment, it is tempting to give up our hope for a brighter tomorrow. Although we may lose sight of our vision momentarily, we need not despair. Scripture reminds us that those who trust in the Lord will not be disappointed. God promises to renew the hope of those who are willing to trust in Him and seek his guidance.

CALCULATED RISKS

ooooooooooooooooooooooooooooooooo

Change and growth take place when a person has risked himself and dares to become involved with experimenting with his own life.

—Herbert Otto

I once saw a T-shirt which had the following inscription printed on the back: "I would be willing to risk almost anything in life except not ever having lived my dreams." There is nothing wrong with taking some calculated risks. Desperate times may require some risk taking. For example, it may be necessary to make major career changes, go back to school or take a lesser paying job for the time being.

Of course, decisions should be made with sound motives and consideration for the well-being of yourself and those closest to you. Consider carefully the possible outcomes of your choices. Be willing to live with the consequences if your plans don't work out. There is nothing wrong with betting on yourself and the future if you are willing to work hard toward fulfilling your dreams.

VOCATIONAL QUEST

○ ○

The years forever fashion new dreams when old ones go. God pity the one-dream man.

—*space scientist, Robert Goddard*

Recent research on the opinions of college freshmen indicates they want to get an education and then get out and make lots of money. With the high cost of schooling such attitudes may be understandable. Still, it's too bad. Whatever happened to their desire to help those who are less fortunate? What about the development of a sound philosophy of life?

Author Sam Keen believes we organize our lives too much around jobs and money. He feels this over-preoccupation becomes ridiculous when carried too far. Keen, who resigned a full professorship to seek a new vocation, believes people must ask themselves two important questions: "What are my gifts and how can I best use them to live a fulfilling life?" Once a person has examined his skills and dreams, he is then ready to ask, "What do I want to do in order to make my living?"

Sometimes our dreams are too narrow. God wants to stretch us to fit a broader vision that involves more than simply serving our own limited interests. He wants us to grow into the kind of person He can use for his purposes. Praying daily for knowledge of God's will and the power to carry it out is a good way to begin the process of broadening our vision. Remember, God is more interested in the kind of person you are than your line of work.

DEALING WITH CHANGE

o o o o o o o o o o o o o o o o o o o o o o o o o o o o o o o o o o o

In times of change, learners inherit the earth, while the learned find themselves beautifully equipped to deal with a world that no longer exists.

—Eric Hoffer

Today, the phrase "life long learning" is frequently heard in any discussion with regard to career maintenance. It is taken for granted that one's employability rests on his or her willingness to keep up their skills and continue learning throughout their career life. The key to successful steady, long term employment is to keep as many job options open as possible for as long as possible. It sounds overwhelming doesn't it? It needn't be if we are willing to stay current in our field and keep alert to the changes in the world around us.

Persons who master change utilize opportunities to sharpen their job skills. They are constantly striving to broaden their knowledge. People who master change are not defensive about helping fellow workers. They are team players who welcome the opportunity work with others toward common goals.

Adaptability is the key to navigating career changes in our ever-changing world. By accepting rather than fighting the necessity of change, you can enhance your chances of staying employed. You can begin today by making a commitment to become a life long learner.

ARE YOU STILL LOOKING FOR WORK?

o o o o o o o o o o o o o o o o o o o o o o o o o o o o o o o o

There is much to do and so many ways to work to combat the ills of the world...There is a whole world out there just waiting for you—waiting and needing—to make use of your resources and the work of your hands.

—From the book, "Business Bible" by Wayne Dosick

Every now and then a jobless person needs to ask: "Am I still looking for work?" I know the answer will be a vehement "yes!" in most cases. But the fact remains that we sometimes give up searching for work without knowing it. We have gotten so accustomed to looking for our specialty or our ideal job that we lose sight of the fact that we need to be working. We are so involved in just making job contacts that we forget what's important. In the end we may become too selective for our own good. If you have been out of work for a while, it may be time for a reality check. It begins by honestly appraising your present situation. If your job expectations are too high, you may have to set your sights a little lower to find work. There is nothing wrong with working at a short term job until something more promising comes along.

NEVER SAY NEVER

Years ago, I worked my way through college as a butcher in a small grocery store. One task I hated was leaning over backwards to clean the glass inside a twelve-foot meat counter. I swore if I could just get through college I would never do that kind of back breaking work again. A few years later I was taking graduate course work in another part of the country. I needed a job that would free up my day time for classes and library research. I applied at a large supermarket meat department for a late night clean-up job. Fortunately, the manager needed some help due to a recent resignation. He showed me the tables and pans that he expected me to scrub. He pointed out several electric saws that would have to be broken down and washed. Then he led me to a fifty-foot meat counter and said: "I want this counter washed down spotless and thoroughly wiped dry inside and out each night before you leave."

Most of us have had jobs we would just as soon never have to do again. We thought if we could just get that degree or that promotion we would be spared having to do that work ever again. Many of us today are faced with our own fifty-foot meat counter. Today's volatile job market is forcing us to re-examine our rigid announcements about what we will and will not do for a living. Suddenly, flexibility seems a better choice than no choice. As career analyst Carol Kleiman points out, "Flexibility is the key to success in today's volatile job market." According to her, "Flexible means being able to rebound after being downsized or adaptable enough to do all the work in a bare-bones staff." We may even have to take a job with a lesser title or salary. In summing up, Kleiman says, "Being flexible means you're smart enough and secure enough to make a lateral move, to welcome retraining, to go wherever jobs are, or to move from a for-profit to a nonprofit one and vice versa." In essence being flexible in today's job world means having the ability to stay employable no matter what happens. It often means never saying "never" to any job opportunity.

REMEMBERING THOSE WHO DO THE WORK

o o o o o o o o o o o o o o o o o o o o o o o o o o o o o o o o

Work without grumbling or getting into disputes.

—*Ephesians 6: 7 NAS*

We may forget how many of our fellow countrymen punch a time clock. We forget how many workers never get a two-day week end off to be with their families because their time off is always split up. We forget how many work for a bare minimum wage without vacation time and sick leave. We overlook how many jobs involve long hard hours where one stands on his or her feet most of the day. We forget how many jobs involve back breaking and even dangerous labor. We forget these things so easily, unless of course we are doing one of those jobs.

It's difficult to take a job that we feel is beneath our dignity. It's like starting again, learning the same difficult lessons. Yet it is not quite the same. Each new job requires new attitudes and skills. The attitude of willingness makes things go more smoothly. When we are willing to do the work without murmuring or complaint, our labor naturally flows better. Learning new tasks and relearning old ones is not so much of a chore when our attitude is one of willingness and gratitude. Pray for the willingness to be willing today.

WORKING OUTSIDE YOUR FIELD

○ ○

Thank God every morning when you have something to do which must be done whether you like it or not. Being forced to work and forced to do your best will breed in your temperament self control, diligence, strength of will and a hundred other virtues which the idle never know.

—*Charles Kingsley*

There are three things working outside your career field can teach you:

1. There is dignity in almost all kinds of labor.

2. There is something to be learned from almost any job.

3. There is gratitude for having some form of purposeful employment once again.

It's hard taking on a job you're not sure you really want. Do it anyway, if you are offered the opportunity. The self discipline of being back on a job will do you good, and perhaps it will lead to something better. A job of any kind can often lead to a more promising type of work. You may even learn some valuable skills that will be useful later on in life. Almost any job can teach something of value if we let it.

So, look upon any work as an opportunity not to be refused. Do your best on the new job and labor without complaint. In the meantime, you can still continue your search for something more suitable with a new self assuredness that says, "I'm not afraid to work. I still have what it takes to handle whatever life throws at me."

RETURNING TO WORK

o o o o o o o o o o o o o o o o o o o o o o o o o o o o o o o o o
The work will teach you how to do it.

—Estonian Proverb

Starting back to work after a long siege of unemployment may cause you to panic. For so long you feared that you would never find work. Now you worry about the impending demands on your life. Sometimes you even start doubting whether you belong in your new job. Such fears are normal. After being inactive for a long period it is only natural to feel a little threatened by new routines and job expectations. When panic threatens, just remember, you have survived job learning experiences before and you will conquer these as well. You don't have to know everything at once and most fellow employees will help you if you ask them. Finally, recognize that every employee who works with you was once where you are today, starting out. So be patient with yourself and thankful for the job. Eventually you will master your new position.

CAREER CHANGE

A major career change is difficult at any age. The problem with change is that it disturbs our set pattern of thinking and acting. Suddenly we are forced into new ways of living. Not only must we act out new roles, we must also learn new methods of problem solving. Fortunately, in most instances we are able to build on past learning experiences so that we already have a start in establishing a successful foundation for our new job. If we approach each new task with confidence and enthusiasm, we soon become able to master most of them.

Recalling past victories over life adjustments can help you proceed with a winning attitude of confidence. Winners have a plan for the future. They are willing to work hard to master the demands of their new job. They set high standards for the quality of their workmanship. They get enthusiastic about their goals and are not easily discouraged. You can give yourself permission to be a winner today.

MISSING THE BLESSINGS
OF LIFE

○ ○

Misfortune can make or break us, depending on how we take it…Suffering accepted may place us in a more advanced position in our career and give us a serenity which may well prove to be our most rewarding experience.

—From "Words of Comfort" by Paul S. Mc Elroy

Every time of trial in life has its blessing for us. Sometimes we miss the blessings of life's difficulties because we focus only on the negative aspects of our hardships. On the surface, lengthy periods of unemployment may seem bleak and meaningless. In truth, we cannot know the full meaning of any single period in relation to the whole of our existence. Like a weaving when viewed from the underside, the pattern may seem disjointed and meaningless. Yet if we could see the top side, we would be amazed at the overall beauty and integrity of the design.

The fact is that being unemployed can be one of the most difficult periods a person faces in life. Fortunately, we find that these tough times do not last and that we do have the capabilities and resources to survive. In looking back, we see that jobless times were often blessings in disguise. If we remain positive in our outlook, we can emerge from our struggle with a new vision for our life and the future.

LESSONS LEARNED

○ ○

Trust in the Lord with all your heart and lean not on your own understanding; in all your ways acknowledge him, and He will make your paths straight.

—Proverbs 3: 5-6 NIV

While times between jobs have been difficult, they have not been without lasting benefit. Hard times teach us the value of living on a budget and saving for a rainy day. Being out of work reinforces our on-going need to be self disciplined and organized in the use of time and money.

The daily struggle to find work also teaches us patience and humility in our relationships. In time we come to realize just how much we need the love and support of others. As we are forced to simplify our life, we come to see that relationships with others are what really matter in life.

A period of belt tightening shows us that we really don't need many material things to be contented. Learning to make do with what we have can be truly enlightening. In time, we come to understand that we are tougher and more resilient than we realized. Just knowing we possess the coping skills necessary to survive gives us a renewed sense of confidence and pride in ourselves.

Finally, living on the edge helps reinforce our need to trust in the guidance of God. There is nothing like having to live one day at a time with the uncertainty of joblessness to teach us the meaning of faith. When we learn to accept God's guidance, we find the path to a deeper faith. A true sense of serenity comes from knowing we can trust in Him.

RECESSION-PROOFING YOUR CAREER

What I learn no one can take away from me.

—*Danish Proverb*

Experts in employment counseling tell us that job security in America no longer exists. This is hardly news to most American workers. Even before the present economic slow-down, there was a growing realization that long-term employment for many of us was becoming a thing of the past. While there are no guarantees that you won't ever be unemployed again, there are some precautions you can take in dealing with your own job uncertainties.

1. Continue your education and training in your field whenever possible.

2. Master computer and other job related skills.

3. Continue networking with other persons in your field.

4. Keep your resume updated.

5. Stay alert to what is happening in your field and the general economy.

6. Save for future emergencies just in case you are laid off again.

The lessons we have learned from our unemployment experiences can benefit us in the future. We can begin now to simplify our lives and learn to live within our means. Most importantly, we continue working to develop a stronger relationship with God. There is no better insurance against uncertain times.

GOD'S GUIDELINES FOR HIS WORKERS

o o o o o o o o o o o o o o o o o o o o o o o o o o o o o o o o o

With good will render services, as to the Lord and not unto men.

—Ephesians 6: 7 NAS

While there may be little job security these days, there are still steps you can take to improve your chances of staying employed. The Bible is filled with stories and recommendations regarding the kind of workers God would have His people be. Following these guidelines can help insure that you will be a valued employee whose work is prized by your employer.

1. Work without grumbling or getting into disputes. (Philippians 2: 14)

2. Conduct yourself in a way that will bring a spirit of peace and gentleness to others on the job. (Galatians 5: 22-23)

3. Pay attention to the details of your job and use your time wisely. (Ephesians 5: 15-16)

4. Work with prayer and petition in behalf of others. (1 Timothy 2: 1)

5. Be wise in the way you act toward fellow workers. Encourage and help those around you. (Colossians 4: 6)

6. Commit your work to the Lord and your plans will prosper. (Proverbs 16:3)

It is God who grounds our work in His purpose. Only God can bless your work and make it a blessing to others.

FINAL THOUGHTS

o o o o o o o o o o o o o o o o o o o o o o o o o o o o o o o o o o o o o
Praise be to the God and Father of our Lord Jesus Christ, the Father of compassion and the God of all comfort, who comforts us in all our troubles so that we can comfort those in any trouble with the comfort we ourselves have received from God.

—2 Corinthians 1: 3-4 NIV

Those of us who have gone through a lengthy period of unemployment are apt to feel remorseful and abused. It takes time to settle all the mixed feelings of frustration. We keep asking ourselves what was all that about and why did I have to go through such turmoil? There are no simple answers to such questions. As an old Burmese proverb states, "suffering is a promise life always keeps." I suppose that is correct. Even the Bible tells us that life is hard.

I believe human suffering does have its purpose in life. It humbles us and makes us more understanding of those who face similar ordeals. It can make us less apt to take God's blessings for granted. Hardships often force us into a deeper, more dependent relationship with Him.

In the end we may never quite understand why our job loss had to happen to us or why our struggle to find work took so long. Still we must trust that God can and will bring good out of the evil that befalls his people. There can be no greater good than that we would be willing to reach out to help others in their time of need. By assisting others with their burdens, we facilitate our own healing as well as theirs.

0-595-33069-X

Printed in the United States
144312LV00010B/18/A